FOCUS

POWERED BY

Practice
Tests Plus

EXAM PRACTICE

CAMBRIDGE ENGLISH **FIRST**

Pearson Education Limited
Edinburgh Gate
Harlow
Essex CM20 2JE
and Associated Companies throughout the world.

www.pearsonelt.com/exams

First published 2016
ISBN: 978-1-292-12116-1

Fourth impression 2018
4

Set in Arial
Printed and bound by CPI Group (UK) Ltd, Croydon, CR0 4YY

Text acknowledgements
Extract Test 1, Part.1 adapted from "What's so bad about comfort eating?",
The Financial Times, 01/12/2012, p.59 (Julian Baggini and Antonia Macaro),
copyright © The Financial Times Limited 2012. All Rights Reserved; Extract on pages
14-15 adapted from "I indexed Shanghai's soup dumplings", *The Financial Times*,
12/06/2015 (Christopher St Cavish as told to Natalie Whittle), copyright © The
Financial Times Ltd 2015. All Rights Reserved; Extract Test 1, Part.7 adapted from
"The secret of my success: How five high-flying graduates made it", *The Independent*,
27/08/2011, p.10 (Holly Williams), copyright (c) The Independent, www.independent.
co.uk; Extract Test 2, Part.5 adapted from "The Original Olympic Hero", *The Financial
Times*, 27/07/2012, p.7 (Simon Kuper), copyright © The Financial Times Limited
2012. All Rights Reserved; Extract on pages 36-37 adapted from "I hunted down my
grandfather's paintings", *The Financial Times*, 03/07/2015 (Robert Seyffert as told to
John O'Connor), copyright © The Financial Times Ltd 2015. All Rights Reserved

Photo acknowledgements
The publisher would like to thank the following for their kind permission to reproduce
their photographs:

(Key: b-bottom; c-centre; l-left; r-right; t-top)

123RF.com: 49b; **Alamy Images:** Design Pics Inc 53t, Chad Ehlers 53b;
Corbis: arabianEye / Celia Peterson 50t, Blend Images / Moxie Productions 49t;
Fotolia.com: Kadmy 52b; **Getty Images:** David Grossman 52t;
Pearson Education Ltd: 55; **Shutterstock.com:** Monkey Business Images 50b

All other images © Pearson Education

Contents

Exam Overview

The **Cambridge English: First** exam, also known as the **First Certificate in English (FCE)** is made up of four papers, each testing a different area of ability in English. The Reading and Use of English paper carries 40% of the marks, while Writing, Listening and Speaking each carry 20% of the marks. There are three grades: A, B and C.

Reading and Use of English	1 hour 15 minutes
Writing	1 hour 20 minutes
Listening	40 minutes (approximately)
Speaking	14 minutes (for each pair of students)

All the examination questions are task-based. Rubrics (instructions) are important and should be read carefully. They set the context and give important information about the tasks. There is a separate answer sheet for recording answers for the Reading and Use of English and Listening papers.

Paper	Format	Task focus
Reading and Use of English 7 tasks, 52 questions	**Part 1:** multiple-choice cloze Choosing which word from a choice of four fits in each of eight gaps in the text.	Choice of vocabulary and relationships between words.
	Part 2: open cloze Writing the missing word in each of eight gaps in the text.	Grammar, vocabulary and knowledge of expressions.
	Part 3: word formation Choosing the form of the word given so that it fits into the gap in the text, with a total of eight gaps.	Grammatical accuracy and knowledge of vocabulary and expressions.
	Part 4: key word transformations Using a key word to complete a new sentence which means the same as the one given, with a total of six sentences.	Grammatical accuracy and knowledge of vocabulary and sentence structure.
	Part 5: multiple choice Answering six four-option multiple-choice questions based on a text.	Reading for detailed understanding of the text.
	Part 6: gapped text Choosing sentences to fit into six gaps in a text.	Reading to understand text structure.
	Part 7: multiple matching Deciding which of the short extracts or paragraphs contains given information or ideas and matching these with ten questions.	Reading to locate specific information, detail, opinion and attitude.

Paper	Format	Task focus
Writing 2 tasks	**Part 1:** compulsory task Using given information to write an essay of 140–190 words.	Focus on writing for an English teacher in a formal style.
	Part 2: producing one piece of writing of 140–190 words, from a choice of the following: a letter/email, a report, a review or an article.	Focus on writing for a specific target reader, using appropriate layout and register.
Listening 4 tasks, 30 questions	**Part 1:** multiple choice Eight short recordings each with a three-option multiple-choice question.	Understanding gist, detail, function, purpose, attitude, etc.
	Part 2: sentence completion One long recording with ten sentence-completion questions.	Locating and recording specific information.
	Part 3: multiple matching Set of five short recordings all related to the same theme to match to one of eight prompts.	Understanding gist and main points.
	Part 4: multiple choice One long recording with seven three-option multiple-choice questions.	Understanding attitude, opinion, gist, main ideas and specific information.
Speaking 4 tasks	**Part 1:** examiner-led conversation	Giving personal information.
	Part 2: individual long turn with visual and written prompts	Organising discourse, describing, comparing and giving opinions.
	Part 3: two-way collaborative task with written prompts	Sustaining interaction, expressing, justifying and eliciting ideas, agreeing and disagreeing.
	Part 4: three-way examiner-led discussion	Expressing and justifying ideas, agreeing and disagreeing.

Practice Test 1 with Guidance

Parts 1–4

About the paper

The *Reading and Use of English* paper lasts for 1 hour and 15 minutes. It contains seven parts, and has a total of fifty-two questions. There are texts of varying lengths, with a range of text types and styles of writing, for example extracts from newspapers, magazines, websites and novels. The paper tests your knowledge of vocabulary and grammar as well as your ability to read and understand a range of texts.

Part 1: Multiple-choice cloze

In Part 1, you read a short text and complete a multiple-choice cloze task. Eight words or phrases have been removed from the text. For each gap, you have to choose from four options the word or phrase which fits best.

Part 2: Open cloze

In Part 2, you read a short text and complete an open cloze task. Eight words have been removed from the text. You have to complete the gaps.

Part 3: Word formation

In Part 3, you read a short text and complete a word formation task. Eight words have been removed from the text. You are given the base form of each missing word and you have to put that word into the correct form to fit the gap.

Part 4: Key word transformation

In Part 4, you read six pairs of sentences and complete a key word transformation task. The pairs of sentences have the same meaning, but are expressed in different ways. Two to five words have been removed from the second sentence, and one of these words, the key word, is given as a prompt. You have to complete the second sentence, using the key word.

How to do the paper

Part 1

- Read the text through once, ignoring the gaps, to get a general understanding.
- Only one of the options (A–D) fits the gap.
- Check the words before and after the gap, e.g. some words can only be followed by a particular preposition.
- Some questions focus on linking words and so test your understanding of the whole sentence or passage.
- If you are not sure which word to choose, decide which options are clearly wrong, and then see which options are left. If you're still not sure, you should guess. You do not lose marks for wrong answers and your guess may be right!
- When you have finished, read the completed text again and check that it makes sense.

Part 2

- Read the text through once, ignoring the gaps, to get a general understanding.
- Think about the missing words. Each gap only needs one word, usually a grammatical word, e.g. a pronoun, a linker, a preposition, etc. The gaps will not test your knowledge of topic vocabulary.
- Carefully read the text around each gap and think about what type of word is missing, e.g. a preposition, a pronoun, part of a fixed expression, etc.
- When you have finished, read the completed text again and check that it makes sense.

Part 3

- Read the text through once, ignoring the gaps, to get a general understanding.
- Decide which type of word is needed in each gap, e.g. a noun, an adjective, an adverb or a verb. Look at the whole sentence, not just at the line including the gap.
- Look at the word in capitals to the right of the gap. You may need to add a prefix or suffix, or make other changes. More than one change may be required.
- Check to see if nouns should be singular or plural.
- When you have finished, read the completed text again and check that it makes sense.

Part 4

- Read through the first sentence.
- Look at the key word. What type of word is it? What usually follows it, e.g. an infinitive, a preposition, or could it be part of a phrasal verb?
- Think about the other words that need to change in the new sentence, e.g. an adjective may become a noun or vice versa.
- Your answer may include words or expressions not used in the first sentence, but these must express exactly the same idea. Do not include new information or change the information.
- Remember that contracted words count as two words, e.g. *won't = will not*.

Parts 5–7

About the paper

Part 5: Multiple choice

In Part 5, there is one long text to read. You have to answer six four-option, multiple-choice questions, which follow the order of the text.

Part 6: Gapped text

In Part 6, there is one long text from which six sentences have been removed. These are placed in jumbled order after the text along with an extra sentence that does not fit into any of the gaps. You have to use your knowledge of grammar, vocabulary, referencing and text structure to reconstruct the text.

Part 7: Multiple matching

In Part 7, there is either one long text that has been divided into sections, or a series of short texts on the same topic. There are also ten prompts which report information and ideas from the text(s). You have to match each prompt to the correct text or section of text.

How to do the paper

Part 5

- Read the text quickly to get a general understanding of what it's about and how it's organised.

- Read through the questions or question stems without looking at the options (A–D), and underline key words in the question stem.

- The questions follow the order of the text. Find the piece of text where a question is answered and read it carefully, underlining key words and phrases.

- Some questions which test vocabulary or reference skills will tell you on which line the targeted word or phrase can be found. Read the sentences before and after the one including this word or phrase to find the answer.

- Try to answer the question. Then read the four options (A–D) and choose the one that is closest to your own answer. Look for the same meaning expressed in different ways.

- Check that the other options are all clearly wrong. If you are still unsure, read the text again very carefully and look for reasons why some of the options may be wrong.

Part 6

- Read the base text first, ignoring the gaps, to get a general understanding of what it's about and how it's organised.

- Next, carefully read the text around each gap and think about what type of information might be missing.

- Read sentences A–G. Check for topic and language links with the base text. Highlight reference words and words that relate to people, places, events and any time references. This will help you follow the development of the argument or narrative.

- Choose the best option to fit each gap. Make sure that all the pronouns and vocabulary references are clear.

- Once you've finished, re-read the completed text to be sure that it makes sense with the answers in the gaps.

Part 7

- In Part 7, you don't need to read the whole text or texts first. The text contains some information that you don't need to answer the questions.

- Read the prompts (43–52) first, underlining key words and ideas.

- Read through the text(s) quickly and find information or ideas that relate to each question.

- For each question, when you find the relevant piece of text, read it very carefully to make sure it completely matches the meaning of the prompt.

- The ideas in each prompt are likely to occur in more than one section of the text, but only one text exactly matches the idea. You need to read all these sections carefully.

Part 1

For questions **1–8**, read the text below and decide which answer (**A**, **B**, **C** or **D**) best fits each gap. There is an example at the beginning (**0**).

In the exam, you mark your answers **on a separate answer sheet**.

Example:

0 **A** come **B** reached **C** found **D** arrived

0	A	B	C	D
	▬	▭	▭	▭

Tip strip

Question 2: Which of these adverbs means 'just a little bit'?

Question 4: Which of these words is normally used to talk about the results of 'research'?

Question 7: Look at the sentence after the gap and think about the meaning. Which word will provide the contrast here?

Question 8: Which of these verbs collocates with the preposition 'on'?

Chocolate is good for you

I was delighted to read recently that various researchers have **(0)** .... to the conclusion that eating chocolate can bring both physical and psychological health **(1)** .... What a relief! I've always felt **(2)** .... guilty about turning to chocolate to cheer myself up when I feel unhappy or under **(3)** .... What's more, chocolate is perfect when I want to treat myself or if I have something to celebrate.

If I looked behind the headlines, however, I'm sure I'd find that the **(4)** .... of the research are more complicated than that. The kinds of foods that we usually **(5)** .... with comfort eating tend to be fatty and sugary and chocolate is no **(6)** .... to this rule. So I imagine that the researchers are talking about eating chocolate in moderation. So I shall continue to watch how much of it I eat! **(7)** .... enjoying chocolate certainly helps to improve my mood in the short-term, coming to **(8)** .... on it too much wouldn't be such a good idea.

1	**A**	aids	**B**	benefits	**C**	advantages	**D**	gains
2	**A**	widely	**B**	slightly	**C**	hardly	**D**	surely
3	**A**	worry	**B**	nerves	**C**	pressure	**D**	problems
4	**A**	details	**B**	items	**C**	matters	**D**	issues
5	**A**	regard	**B**	join	**C**	associate	**D**	concern
6	**A**	comparison	**B**	exception	**C**	difference	**D**	alternative
7	**A**	Whilst	**B**	Despite	**C**	Nonetheless	**D**	Given
8	**A**	commit	**B**	confide	**C**	trust	**D**	rely

Tip strip

Question 9: A relative pronoun is needed here – it links the idea to the place.

Question 10: Which word will follow on from 'either' earlier in the sentence?

Question 11: Which preposition completes this linking phrase?

Question 14: You are looking for the word that follows 'rather'.

Question 15: Which adverb is used to link these two ideas?

For questions **9–16**, read the text below and think of the word which best fits each gap. Use only **one** word in each gap. There is an example at the beginning (**0**).

In the exam, you write your answers **IN CAPITAL LETTERS on a separate answer sheet**.

Example: | 0 | B | Y | | | | | | | | | | | | | | | | | | | | | | |

In search of silence

When city dwellers go deep into the countryside, they are often struck (**0**) .... the wonderful quality of silence. They compare this with the city, (**9**) .... it is never completely quiet. Even in the middle of the night, you can hear either the distant hum of traffic (**10**) .... the buzz coming from streetlights, air-conditioning units and heating systems. The city never sleeps, and its citizens never fully relax.

Of course, the countryside isn't a completely silent place. (**11**) .... the contrary, there are noises all around – birds sing, insects buzz and the wind whistles through the trees. The thing (**12**) .... the countryside is that against the general backdrop of silence, these sounds can be heard so clearly (**13**) .... we're actually able to appreciate them. Rather (**14**) .... irritating us when it breaks the silence, birdsong is perceived (**15**) .... beautiful. We go to the countryside in (**16**) .... to find peace, and the sounds of the countryside are as much a part of that as the silence itself.

Tip strip

Question 17: You need to add two suffixes to this word to create an adverb.

Question 19: Read the paragraph to check whether you need to create a positive or a negative word here.

Question 21: Read the sentence to see if you need to create a singular or plural word.

Question 24: Add a suffix to create the noun from this verb.

Part 3

For questions **17–24**, read the text below. Use the word given in capitals at the end of some of the lines to form a word that fits in the gap **in the same line**. There is an example at the beginning (**0**).

In the exam, you write your answers **IN CAPITAL LETTERS on a separate answer sheet**.

Example: | 0 | U | S | E | F | U | L | | | | | | | | | | | | | | | | | | |

The selfie stick

The selfie stick is a (**0**) .... gadget, which allows us to take	USE
self-portraits with a mobile phone by (**17**) .... providing the	EFFECT
user with an (**18**) .... to their arm. The idea of taking	EXTEND
self-portraits with a camera isn't a new one. As long ago as	
1983, a stick designed to hold a camera for this purpose was	
already on sale. For some (**19**) .... reason, however, the	KNOW
idea failed to catch on. (**20**) .... where the idea of the	EXACT
modern-day selfie stick came from remains something of	
a mystery. Although it featured in *Time Magazine*'s list of the	
twenty-five best (**21**) .... of 2014, something similar had	INVENT
been on sale in the USA since 2011. For a couple of years,	
nobody much noticed its (**22**) .... , then gradually the idea	EXIST
started to gain in (**23**) .... By 2014, it had become a craze.	POPULAR
Suddenly everyone was taking selfies and the sticks were on	
sale at tourist (**24**) .... worldwide.	ATTRACT

Tip strip

Question 25: Think about what form of the verb follows the phrase 'don't mind'.

Question 26: 'allowed' is followed by the infinitive with 'to'.

Question 28: You need to create a phrasal verb with 'after' that means the same as 'take care of'.

Question 29: Pay attention to the period of time mentioned in the first sentence.

For questions **25–30**, complete the second sentence so that it has a similar meaning to the first sentence, using the word given. **Do not change the word given.** You must use between **two** and **five** words, including the word given. Here is an example (**0**).

Example:

0   What type of music do you like best?

   FAVOURITE

   What .... type of music?

The gap can be filled with the words 'is your favourite', so you write:

Example: | **0** | IS YOUR FAVOURITE

In the exam, you write **only** the missing words **IN CAPITAL LETTERS on a separate answer sheet**.

---

25   I'm happy to take you to work in the car.
   LIFT
   I don't mind .... to work.

26   Students must remain in the building at break time.
   ALLOWED
   Students .... leave the building at break time.

27   'I think you should buy yourself a new jacket, Mark,' said Judith.
   ADVISED
   Judith .... a new jacket.

28   You can use my tablet, but you must take good care of it.
   LONG
   You can use my tablet .... after it carefully.

29   The team hasn't won a trophy in years.
   LAST
   It's .... won a trophy.

30   It was the most delicious meal I had ever eaten.
   NEVER
   I .... delicious meal.

Part 5

You are going to read an extract from a novel in which a young man called James is setting off on a journey. For questions **31–36**, choose the answer (**A**, **B**, **C** or **D**) which you think fits best according to the text.

In the exam, you mark your answers **on a separate answer sheet**.

As the car pulled into the airport, James' father picked up their earlier conversation: 'Are you sure you wouldn't rather I parked somewhere and came to see you off properly?' They'd been over this several times. James was meeting the other two volunteers at the bag-drop desk – it had all been arranged by text message. He didn't want his dad around, fretting about the weight of his rucksack. 'No Dad – it's OK,' he said, 'I've got the briefing meeting to attend. You head back home.' James felt a slight pang at misleading his father, but it was a sort of meeting.

James went through the automatic doors and joined other passengers gazing up at the monitor in the entrance hall. There it was JJ435 to Matarma – on time, bag-drop desk 25. Juliet had been the one to suggest meeting up in this way. Wildco, the wildlife organisation, had actually briefed the three student volunteers separately about the survey they'd be carrying out on the island. None of them was studying a relevant subject, so they'd mostly be doing routine tasks under supervision.

Realising they'd all be on the same flight, however, Juliet had suggested travelling together. 'It seems daft being on the same plane and only meeting up once we get there,' she'd said in her text. She had a point of course, so James had gone along with the idea. But when Clive, the third volunteer, hadn't replied at once, she'd resent the message with a red flag and exclamation mark attached. James smiled when he remembered Clive's cool reply: 'I'll think about it and let you know.' Why hadn't he thought of that instead of meekly going along with her suggestion?

'You must be James,' said a voice behind him. He spun round and there she was. Shorter and prettier than he'd expected from the photograph that she'd sent through, she was dragging behind her the largest suitcase on wheels he'd ever seen. 'That's right – and you must be Juliet. Do you want a hand with that?' He asked pointing to the suitcase. 'Certainly not,' she replied smiling, 'I'm quite capable.'

'Yes, of course. Sorry.'

'Where I may need your help though, is if they make a fuss about the weight when we get to the desk. Have you got any space in yours?'

'Umm I don't know really …'

'… and before you ask, I don't do rucksacks because they're bad for your back.'

'Oh, right.'

'Great. It doesn't look like twenty kilos worth to me. So I'm sure we'll work something out.'

'Oh I didn't mean …' James hesitated. Juliet gave him a quizzical look – one he was going to see time
line 30   and again during the next six weeks. 'Never mind,' he said smiling weakly. 'That'll be fine.'

'I do hope we're going to get on, James. Because I'm a bit worried about Clive.'

'Really?'

'Daniela at Wildco said he was having second thoughts about the whole trip.'

'Really – she didn't say anything to me.'

'Well no – it's not official or anything – she was just tipping me off, you know. I was at school with her, actually.'

'Oh right.'

At that point their conversation was interrupted by a loud ringtone coming from Juliet's suitcase. She plucked a smartphone out of a side-pocket.

'Well!' She exclaimed, 'it seems I was wrong. It's Clive. He says "See you in the departure lounge – I've got no bag – I always travel light." But I distinctly said to meet at the bag drop.' Juliet suddenly looked
line 42   rather crestfallen. James almost felt sorry for her until she added: 'In that case, we're going to need all the spare space in your rucksack, James. Come on – let's get moving.'

Tip strip

Question 31: The answer is in the first paragraph. Look for the sentence beginning, 'James felt a slight pang ...'. Which answer option has the idea of 'misleading' somebody?

Question 33: Look for his first reaction – not what he thought later.

Question 35: Look back in the text to find what James is referring to here. You need to go back to the beginning of their conversation.

31 From the first paragraph, we understand that James felt

   A grateful to his father for the lift to the airport.

   B irritated by his father's attitude towards the trip.

   C guilty at not having told his father the complete truth.

   D touched that his father wanted to wait with him in the airport.

32 Why were the three students travelling to the island?

   A to take part in a research project

   B to do paid work for a wildlife charity

   C to observe the work of a voluntary organisation

   D to fulfil the requirements of their course of study

33 How did James initially regard Juliet's suggestion that they meet at the airport?

   A He was suspicious of her motives.

   B He thought it was a reasonable idea.

   C He regarded it as rather inconvenient.

   D He was surprised the organisers hadn't arranged it.

34 From the group's exchange of text messages, James gained the impression that Clive

   A seemed to be rather rude.

   B had a good sense of humour.

   C was a rather unpredictable character.

   D liked to make up his own mind about things.

35 The word 'that' in line 30 refers to

   A a request for help.

   B a piece of luggage.

   C a future relationship.

   D a measure of weight.

36 What does the word 'crestfallen' in line 42 suggest about Juliet?

   A She was angry about something.

   B She was disappointed at the turn of events.

   C She was determined to go through with her plans.

   D She was easily upset if people were unkind to her.

You are going to read an article by a food writer about a kind of Asian food called 'soup dumplings'. Six sentences have been removed from the article. Choose from the sentences **A–G** the one which fits each gap (37–42). There is one extra sentence you do not need to use.

In the exam, you mark your answers **on a separate answer sheet.**

In search of the perfect dumpling

My mum was an awful cook and perhaps because of that, I was always interested in food. I got my first job as a washer-up aged fifteen, then I spent ten years as a chef in different parts of the world.

I came to Asia because I wanted to see Chinese and Japanese food first hand. In 2005 I ended up with a job at a French restaurant in Shanghai; the city was really booming, and I was working up to seventy hours a week. **37** So I started to write about Chinese restaurants instead. Soup dumplings were my starting point.

Soup dumplings originated back in the 7ᵗʰ century in central Asia. The idea spread outwards from there, so today you can find something similar almost everywhere from Turkey eastwards. About 150 years ago, they arrived in the Shanghai area of China. **38** In my experience, every region has its own variant on the standard soup dumpling. I thought I'd try and establish what the characteristics of the ideal Shanghai soup dumpling are, then set out to measure those on offer in various city restaurants against that.

When you talk to people from Shanghai, however, they'll always argue about what makes a good soup dumpling. Some will say that the skin must be thin, others that there should be a lot of tasty meat in the filling, or that there must be plenty of soup. **39** So clearly, the perfect dumpling wasn't going to be that easy to find.

Meanwhile, a friend had told me about a guide to restaurants 'prepared for the convenience of mathematicians, experimental scientists, engineers and explorers'. It was the pet project of an eccentric scientist who ate in hundreds of restaurants in New York and then created, by hand, a spreadsheet of them all, using symbols to show the ethnicity of the cuisine, what the place was like, etc. **40** I thought I'd do the same for Shanghai soup dumplings.

I bought a digital scale and a pair of callipers on an internet auction site. With these two tools and a pair of scissors, I went from restaurant to restaurant sampling the soup dumplings. I'd take each one out individually, weigh it and then snip a hole in the side and pour the soup out and weigh that. **41** Using my callipers, I'd then measure the thickness of the skin on the bottom of the dumpling.

I went to around fifty restaurants in all and wouldn't say the family-run places were any worse than the fancy ones with posh tablecloths and uniformed waiters. Hopefully, the guide I have produced will make you laugh and think. **42** On the other hand, it is a list of fifty or so restaurants in Shanghai and it does attempt to put them in some sort of order for you. My next project is shallow-fried dumplings, which are cooked two-hundred at a time. They're a local speciality and incredibly popular.

Tip strip

Question 37: Look for the option that talks about what the writer originally hoped to do in China. The text after the gap describes what he did to achieve his aim.

Question 38: The text before the gap talks about a particular part of the world. Which option starts with a word referring to a place? The text after the gap talks about the way dumplings are made in Shanghai. There are words in the option that describe the food.

Question 41: Look for the option that talks about the next stage in the process.

Question 42: Look for the option that contains a word that refers to 'the guide' before the gap.

A Admittedly, it has nothing to say about taste or texture, which is what people are often interested in.

B Consequently, there was no opportunity to learn about other people's recipes.

C Here they made them a little bit smaller and slightly less sweet than in rival locations.

D I loved how practical, but at the same time completely useless his idea was.

E It was the perfect opportunity to put these theories to the test.

F Then I'd squeeze out the meat and do the same.

G Visiting restaurants, I'd often seen a sign on the wall boasting about these particular qualities in the dumplings on offer.

Tip strip

Question 43: Look in the texts and underline places where family members are mentioned. Which of the graduates is making this point?

Question 44: All the graduates talk about studying or working hard – but which of them mentions a period when they studied less hard?

Question 50: Look for a phrase that describes what a role model is. Only one of the graduates talks about this.

Question 51: 'rule out' means 'decide not to do something'. Which graduate didn't enjoy the work in one job they tried?

Part 7

You are going to read a magazine article about graduates who are just starting their careers after a long period of study. For questions **43–52**, choose from the sections (**A–D**). The sections may be chosen more than once.

In the exam, you mark your answers **on a separate answer sheet**.

Which graduate

acknowledges the positive influence of one family member?   **43** [ ]

admits to not studying particularly hard at one point?   **44** [ ]

chose one place of study because of the atmosphere amongst the students?   **45** [ ]

expresses gratitude for the support of one imaginative individual?   **46** [ ]

feels relatively fortunate compared to some fellow students?   **47** [ ]

mentions being given a time limit within which to accept an offer?   **48** [ ]

praises the attitude of staff in one educational institution?   **49** [ ]

prefers not to be regarded as a role model for other young people?   **50** [ ]

says that one period of work experience helped to rule out a career option?   **51** [ ]

was keen to leave one part of the world as a teenager?   **52** [ ]

Graduate paths

Four recent graduates look back on their educational achievements.

A Hashi

I came to London from East Africa aged nine, without a word of English. I attended an average state school in London. I didn't really pay much attention there, but I scraped through my school leaving exams and got a place at university to study law, though I never really expected to become a lawyer. When I finished, I wrote a cheeky email to the editor of a TV news programme. I told him I had no experience, but wanted to become a journalist. He put me onto a work-placement project, gave me a salary, and let me work on several news programmes. I owe a lot to that man. He was willing to take a chance on me. My story is a combination of people believing in me and having the self-discipline to work very hard. That's not something you can expect from every child however, so it would be unfair to hold me up as an example to follow.

B Amanda

Architecture's always interested me, but my heart wasn't set on it from childhood. I guess it was living in so many different cities that made me appreciate how architecture defines places. I went to high school in Oregon, USA. I studied hard because I knew I wanted to get out of there. I went travelling at the first opportunity. There are no architects in my family, but I learnt the value of hard work from my step-father. I did a foundation art course at a London university, and through that I got myself into the Architectural Association School. It's pretty competitive with only thirty-eight students in my year, but it appealed to me because it's like a close-knit community. Architecture is creative but it's also very rigorous. You have to know the reasoning behind what you do. It takes seven years before you can call yourself an architect, which is a pretty big undertaking.

C Kevin

I never felt any great desire to follow in my father's footsteps and do medicine, though that is the subject I eventually did. Actually, as a teenager, I wanted to join the army because our school had a keen cadet force, and at sixteen I applied and got a place at officer-training college. You have seven years to take the place up before it expires – so there's time to finish school and go to university before starting your army career. I had a great time at university in London. I have a strong work ethic, but I also did other stuff – played rugby, had big nights out. You don't really appreciate how competitive medicine is until you've graduated though – because certain specialisms are really tough to get into, and some people on the course came away disappointed. Luckily, the army is happy for me to specialise in surgery, and I'll be doing that alongside the officer training.

D Marlene

My dad was a journalist – working for German radio in London and Washington when I was a kid. He knew nothing about fashion, but it was living abroad that sparked my interest in the subject. I took sewing lessons from the age of twelve, and it was always more than a hobby. On leaving school, I did an internship at a theatre, doing costume design, but found it wasn't really for me. So I did some drawings and sent them off to Art School in London and got a place there instead. I loved having tutors who knew what they were talking about and really criticised you. As part of the course, I did a couple of three-month internships, including one at a major fashion house, which particularly shaped me. Some of the other interns were a bit half-hearted, or went home early. Not me!

Parts 1 and 2

About the paper

The *Writing* paper lasts for 1 hour and 20 minutes. There are two parts to the paper and in each part you have to complete one task.

Part 1

Part 1 is compulsory. You have to write an essay in a formal style, giving your opinion on the essay title, using the ideas given and providing an idea of your own. You should write between 140 and 190 words.

Part 2

In Part 2, you must choose one question from a choice of three. Tasks may include some of the following: an article, an email, a letter, a report or a review. You should write between 140 and 190 words.

Task types for Part 2

- a letter or an email (formal or informal)
- an article
- a report
- a review

For more information about the writing paper task types, refer to the Writing Bank on pages 59–64.

How to do the paper

Part 1

- Don't be in a hurry to start writing. It pays to spend a few minutes planning! Read the instructions carefully to understand:
  - the topic and the title of the essay you have to write.
  - what information you have to include in your answer: this will ensure that you include the two notes provided.
- Think of a third point of your own, something which is not mentioned in the two points given.
- Look again at the three written notes and expand them by noting down a couple of ideas for each.
- Decide how many paragraphs you will need and which ideas you want to group together in each paragraph.
- When you finish, do a final check. Is the style formal? Have you included all the notes? Are there any basic mistakes that you can correct?

Part 2

- Remember that whereas in Part 1 you always have to write an essay in a formal style, in Part 2 you need to choose from task types that may require a semi-formal or informal style, and a variety of formats.

- Don't be in hurry to start writing. Look carefully at each task (e.g. the report) and topic (e.g. a transport museum) and:
  - think of report writing. Are you confident you know how to write the task type?
  - think of a transport museum as a topic. Do you have some interesting language you can use?
- Choose a topic where your answers to both of the questions above are 'yes'. For example, choose the report only if you know how to present and organise the information, and you also like the topic and have some interesting language you can use.
- Read the task you have chosen and be sure you understand the following:
  - What is the <u>situation</u>?
  - <u>Who</u> will read your piece of writing?
  - What is your <u>purpose</u> in writing this piece?
- Jot down the ideas that come into your head, in any order. Then choose your best ideas and decide how you will organise them into paragraphs.
- When you finish, revise your writing. Have you used varied language? Are your points clearly expressed?

Testing focus

Parts 1 and 2 carry equal marks. Spelling and punctuation, the right length, paragraphing and legible handwriting are taken into account in both parts of the test.

The examiner will consider the following:

content: Have you included all the information required? Is the content of your piece relevant, i.e. are the points clearly connected with the task?

organisation: Have you organised your writing so that the different paragraphs and sentences are connected logically? Have you used a range of linking words and phrases?

language: Have you used a range of language, including varied vocabulary, some complex structures and different tenses?

communicative achievement: Have you communicated your ideas in an effective way, holding the reader's attention?

Part 1

You **must** answer this question. Write your answer in **140–190** words in an appropriate style.

1   In your English class, you have been talking about what it means to be famous and how fame can affect a person's life. Now, your English teacher has asked you to write an essay.

Write an essay using **all** the notes and giving reasons for your point of view.

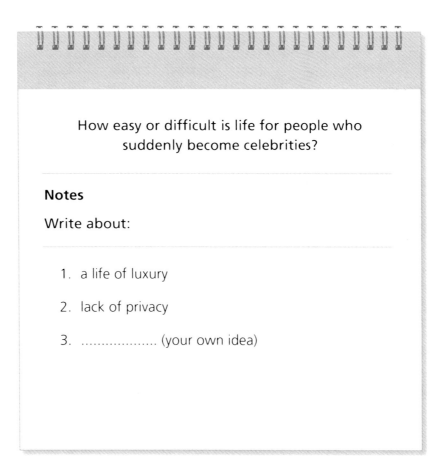

How easy or difficult is life for people who suddenly become celebrities?

Notes

Write about:

1. a life of luxury

2. lack of privacy

3. .... (your own idea)

Tip strip

- Begin by underlining the key words in the instructions, e.g. 'what it means to be famous and how fame can affect a person's life', 'using all the notes'.
- Read the essay question and the two written prompts. Note down a couple of ideas to include for each prompt, and also some interesting vocabulary.

For example, for the first prompt you could jot down 'expensive clothes' or 'glamorous lifestyle'. Think of a third idea of your own and make some notes on that too.

- Spend a few minutes planning your answer. Remember that the time you spend planning your essay is not wasted time! Decide which ideas you will include in each paragraph.

- Introduce the topic in the first paragraph. You can do this by rephrasing the essay question, for example, 'People's lives can change radically when they become celebrities.'

- Use a variety of tenses and grammatical structures and some interesting vocabulary.

- Your final paragraph is important because it is the conclusion of your essay. Summarise the points

you made in previous paragraphs briefly.

- When you have finished, check that you have dealt with the two notes provided and that you have included a point of your own. Check that you have written between 140 and 190 words, but don't waste time counting every word.

- Finally, check your grammar and spelling.

Tip strip

- Read all the questions carefully before choosing one. For example, choose Question 4 if you like writing reports and know some vocabulary related to transport. Before you start writing, think of the task type you have chosen and remember what you have learnt about it.
- Before you start writing, note down the main points you want to include in each paragraph.

Question 2: Write a catchy introduction to get your readers interested. You could use a question, e.g. 'Do you want to learn how to succeed in your studies without getting too stressed? It's not difficult, you only need to …' In paragraph 2, you may want to mention organisation, e.g. making a plan or setting starting and finishing times. In paragraph 3 you could mention breaks, exercise, games, etc. You need to give one extra tip.

Question 3: You're writing to a friend, so your style should be informal. Remember that your email must have opening and closing lines, and that you have to write full sentences. Do not use words that are commonly used in text messages, e.g. 'lol'. Plan your answer: after a brief introduction in paragraph 1 you could mention places to go and the time you have to get back. In paragraph 2 you could mention pocket money or gifts. In the last paragraph, you may want to refer to situations in which parents make decisions.

Question 4: Think of the style needed when you write a report. Underline key words in the task, e.g. 'types of transport', 'liked most and why', 'useful for school work'. Jot down some vocabulary, e.g. *racing cars, buses used last century, space rockets, horse-drawn carriages, films, interactive displays*. You may want to use a heading for each part, but don't forget you will need a short introduction too.

Write an answer to **one** of the questions **2–4** in this part. Write your answer in **140–190** words in an appropriate style.

2 You recently saw this announcement on a teenage website.

Articles wanted!

CAN YOU WRITE AN ARTICLE ON THIS TOPIC AND HELP MILLIONS OF STUDENTS?

How to avoid stress when you're studying hard
- ○ How do you organise your work?
- ○ What do you do to relax?
- ○ What other useful tip do you have to avoid stress?

Write your **article**.

3 You have received an email from your English-speaking friend, Jack, who is doing a presentation at school about teenagers' lives in different parts of the world. Write an email to Jack, answering his questions.

Please tell me how independent teenagers are in your country. Are they allowed to go out alone in the evening? Do they have their own money to spend? How important is it for them to obey their parents?

This will be very useful for my school presentation, thank you!

Please write soon.

Jack

Write your **email**.

4 You recently visited a transport museum with your class. Now your teacher has asked you to write a report covering the following points:

- the types of transport on display
- the sections you and your classmates liked most and why
- how useful this visit was for your school work

Write your **report**.

Parts 1–4

About the paper

The *Listening* paper lasts about 40 minutes and has four parts, with a total of thirty questions. There are recorded texts of varying lengths and types, e.g. extracts from media broadcasts and announcements, as well as everyday conversations. You will hear each recording twice. You have time to read the questions before you listen.

Part 1: Multiple choice

In Part 1, you listen to eight unrelated extracts of around 30 seconds each. The extracts may be monologues or dialogues and will include a range of speakers and contexts. You have to answer one three-option multiple-choice question on each extract. Each question tests a slightly different skill, for example you may be asked to identify a speaker's main point, opinion, feeling or attitude, or whether two speakers agree with each other.

Part 2: Sentence completion

Part 2 involves one long recorded text of around three minutes. You will hear one speaker giving a talk or presentation on a specific topic. Ten sentences report the main points from the listening. A word or short phrase has been removed from each sentence. You have to listen and complete the gaps. This task tests your ability to find and record specific information in the recording.

Part 3: Multiple matching

In Part 3, you hear a series of five short monologues of around 30 seconds each on the same topic. As you listen, you decide which option from a list of eight matches each speaker. This task tests your ability to understand the gist of what people are saying.

Part 4: Multiple choice

In Part 4, there is one long recording of around three minutes. This is generally an interview or a discussion between two people. You have to listen and answer seven three-option multiple-choice questions. This task tests your detailed understanding of the interview, including the main speaker's attitudes, feelings and opinions.

How to do the paper

Part 1

- The eight extracts are not linked in any way.
- Before you listen to each extract, look at the context sentence. Think about who the speaker is and about the context, e.g. is it a broadcast interview, an informal chat?
- Some questions ask you to identify the speakers' opinions. Before you listen, think about which of the speakers you are listening for in each question and underline key words. Some questions focus on whether the speakers agree or not.
- Some questions ask you to identify a speaker's feeling or attitude, or purpose in talking, e.g. to explain, to apologise, etc.
- Some questions test your understanding of a speaker's main idea, or a detailed piece of information that they give.
- Listen first to find the correct answer to the question.
- Listen again to match that answer to the correct option (A–C).

Part 2

- Before you listen, read the rubric and think about the context.
- You have time to read through the sentences before you listen. Think about the type of information that is missing.
- Most answers are concrete pieces of information, e.g. proper nouns or numbers.
- The information on the page follows the same order as the information in the recording. Use the sentences to help you keep your place as you listen.
- The words you need to write are heard on the recording. Don't try to change the form of the words or to find a paraphrase.
- Write no more than three words in each gap. Most answers will be single words or compound nouns.
- Check that your answer fits grammatically, e.g. singular and plural, tense, etc. and that it makes sense in the complete sentence.

Part 3

- There are five different speakers all talking about the same topic. You hear all five of them and then the whole recording is repeated.
- You have time to read the task before you listen. Read options (A–H) so you're ready to choose one as you listen.
- The first time you listen, pay attention to the speaker's main idea. Mark the option closest to this idea. Remember that the five speakers are all talking about the same topic, so you will hear the same vocabulary and similar information.
- The second time you listen, check your answers. You may need to change some of them. Remember that there are three options that you don't need to use.
- Don't worry if you don't understand every word. If you're not sure of an answer, then guess. You have probably understood more than you think.

Part 4

- Before you listen, read the rubric and think about the context.
- You have time to read through the questions before you listen.
- Underline key words in the question stems and options.
- The questions follow the order of the recording. Listen for the interviewer's questions that introduce the topic of each question.
- Listen first to find the correct answer to the question.
- Listen again to match that answer to the correct option (A–C).
- The words in the options may not be the same as those you hear in the recording. Think about the meaning of what the person is saying and the question you're being asked, then find the best match.

Part 1

You will hear people talking in eight different situations. For questions **1–8**, choose the best answer (**A**, **B** or **C**).

Tip strip

Question 1: Listen for the words 'great' and 'livened things up'. What are they talking about when they use these words?

Question 3: Listen for the phrase: 'I wasn't so keen on'. Who or what is the girl referring to when she says this?

Question 5: Listen for a phrase that means 'you should'. The answer comes after it.

Question 7: Listen for a phrase that expresses a similar idea to 'looking forward to'.

1 You hear two friends talking about an end-of-term party.
They agree that the best thing about it was

A the food.

B the venue.

C the music.

2 You hear a sports coach talking to a football team.
He thinks that the team needs to concentrate on their

A attitude towards key matches.

B general physical fitness.

C specific ball skills.

3 You hear two friends talking about a film they have seen.
What does the girl criticise?

A the visual impact

B the choice of actors

C the complexity of the plot

4 You hear a boy talking about a competition he entered.
How does he feel about it?

A disappointed with his performance

B determined to learn from the experience

C dissatisfied with the level of feedback he received

5 You hear a science teacher talking to his class.
What is he doing?

A suggesting the best way to present a piece of work

B advising them how to approach their research

C recommending a useful source of background information

6 You hear a girl leaving a phone message for her friend.
Why is she calling?

A to cancel an appointment

B to rearrange a planned activity

C to apologise for forgetting something

7 You hear a man talking about his holiday plans.
What is he looking forward to most?

A having a break from everyday commitments

B experiencing life in another culture

C trying out some new leisure pursuits

8 You hear two friends discussing traffic problems in their city.
What concerns the girl about priority lanes?

A how much they will cost to install

B whether other road users will respect them

C the effect they will have on levels of congestion

Tip strip

Question 9: You are listening for a sentence which mentions a family member.

Question 12: There are two types of cabin – listen for the name of the type Keith stayed in.

Question 15: Listen for the phrase 'I was cool with that'. It refers to the answer.

Question 16: Be careful, we hear different adjectives that describe the paths and the area.

Question 18: Listen for the word 'overall'. It tells you that Keith is summing up his ideas.

Part 2

You will hear a boy called Keith giving a class presentation about a trip he went on to a place called The Woodland Centre. For questions **9–18**, complete the sentences with a word or short phrase.

The Woodland Centre

Keith's family went to The Woodland Centre on the recommendation of his

(9) ....

Keith was pleased to see some **(10)** ....

in the chill-out room at the centre.

Keith was surprised how far his family's cabin was from the

(11) ....

The cabin which the family stayed in was what's known as a

(12) .... cabin.

Keith thought it was inconvenient that the cabin didn't have a

(13) ....

Keith was pleased to be able to identify some

(14) .... when he was in the hot tub.

Keith was happy with the choice of **(15)** ....

as the group's watersports activity.

Keith was disappointed that the mountain biking activity took place in a

(16) .... area.

Inside the castle they visited, Keith found the

(17) .... the most interesting part.

Keith uses the word **(18)** .... to sum up his

impression of the facilities at the Centre.

Tip strip

Speaker One: Listen for the phrase 'on the panel'. What she says next tells you the answer.

Speaker Two: Listen to what he says about a singer – it helps with the question.

Speaker Three: When he says 'that boy will prove me right', what is he referring to? This helps with the answer.

Speaker Four: Be careful: the audience is mentioned by Speaker 4, but H is not the answer.

Speaker Five: Listen to the first half of what she says. It tells you how she feels about being a judge.

You will hear five short extracts in which people are talking about being a judge in a talent show. For questions **19–23**, choose from the list (**A–H**) how each speaker feels about the experience. Use the letters only once. There are three extra letters which you do not need to use.

A keen to be invited back

Speaker 1 [ ] **19**

B sorry for upsetting one contestant

Speaker 2 [ ] **20**

C unsure whether the best act won

Speaker 3 [ ] **21**

D surprised by the other judges' dedication

Speaker 4 [ ] **22**

E critical of the way it was organised

Speaker 5 [ ] **23**

F pleased to have identified the winner early on

G disappointed by the quality of the acts

H surprised by the behaviour of the audience

Tip strip

Question 24: What does Dan say about his friends? Which option does this refer to?

Question 27: Listen to what Dan says about 'clients' What does he mean by this?

Question 26: Be careful: all three ideas are mentioned. Which one does Dan appreciate 'most'?

Question 29: Listen for the phrase 'And that's what I did.' What does it refer to?

Part 4

You will hear an interview with a successful hairdresser called Dan Shefford. For questions **24–30**, choose the best answer (**A**, **B** or **C**).

24 Dan decided to train as a hairdresser as a result of

   A   encouragement from his parents.

   B   positive feedback on his practical skills.

   C   realising it was a good business to get into.

25 Looking back on his initial training, Dan feels

   A   grateful for the skills he learnt.

   B   embarrassed by the way he behaved.

   C   disappointed by aspects of a course he followed.

26 What did Dan appreciate most about his first job as a fully-trained hairdresser?

   A   the type of clients he got to work with

   B   the attitude of the person in charge

   C   the good reputation it enjoyed

27 Dan thinks that, above all, a good hairdresser needs

   A   a lively imagination.

   B   an interest in developing new styles.

   C   a genuine wish to understand other people.

28 When Dan inherited some money, he felt

   A   unsure what he should do with it.

   B   obliged to follow his uncle's instructions.

   C   keen to use most if it to further his career.

29 How did Dan deal with the challenges of running his own salon?

   A   He got a former boss to give him advice.

   B   He followed the example of someone he admired.

   C   He forced the staff to accept new ways of working.

30 When asked about business skills, Dan says that

   A   he's come to rely on a colleague he can trust.

   B   he finds it hard to accept the advice of experts.

   C   he accepts that they don't come naturally to him.

Parts 1–4

About the paper

The *Speaking* test contains four parts and lasts 14 minutes. There are two candidates and two examiners. One examiner acts as interlocutor and interacts with the candidates and the other examiner acts as assessor and does not join the conversation. The candidates are assessed on grammar and vocabulary, discourse management, pronunciation and interactive communication over the whole test.

Part 1 (2 minutes)

Testing focus: In this part, candidates have to show that they are able to use everyday social and interactional language, such as answering questions about themselves. Examiners will encourage the use of natural language and discourage prepared speeches. Students will need to show an ability to use good basic grammar and a good range of vocabulary.

Procedure: The examiner asks candidates questions about their own lives, focusing on areas such as their daily life, leisure, work, future plans, holidays, likes and dislikes. The examiner addresses each candidate in turn. This is a natural way to begin the test and it allows candidates to settle and feel comfortable.

Part 2 (4 minutes)

Testing focus: This part tests the candidates' ability to speak for one minute without the examiner's support. Candidates have to be able to produce language which fulfils the task they have been given, organising their ideas in such a way as to make it easy to understand. This will require the use of some complex language forms, different tenses, linking words, etc.

Procedure: Each candidate is given the opportunity to speak for one minute without interruption. The examiner gives each candidate two pictures and reads out a task. One part of this task is to compare them, but there is also an extra task which is written above the pictures. At the end of each long turn, the examiner asks the other candidate a question which only requires a brief answer.

Part 3 (4 minutes)

Testing focus: This part tests the candidates' ability to take part in a discussion by initiating, responding to their partner's comments, and inviting their partner's opinions. Candidates will have to express, justify and evaluate different opinions, using language of collaboration and negotiation. There is no right or wrong answer to this task and candidates won't be penalised if they fail to reach a decision.

Procedure: Both candidates are given oral instructions and a diagram with one question and five written prompts. The instructions for this part are in two parts. First the examiner will ask the candidates to talk to each other about the question and the different written prompts. The written question helps candidates focus on the task. The candidates will be given 15 seconds to look at the task before starting the discussion. Then, after two minutes, the examiner will give the candidates one minute to decide on something. When making their decision, candidates will be expected to give reasons for their choices.

Part 4 (4 minutes)

Testing focus: This part tests the candidates' ability to engage in a discussion and to deal with issues in more depth than in earlier parts of the test. Candidates are expected to use a range of grammar and vocabulary when expressing ideas and opinions. They will be assessed on their use of language, not on the opinions they express.

Procedure: The examiner asks the candidates questions related to the points discussed in Part 3, which broaden the topic and allow the candidates to discuss issues in more depth. The examiner will address some questions to both candidates (it does not matter who answers first) and some to each of them individually.

How to do the paper

Part 1

Listen carefully to the examiner's questions and to your partner's answers, as you might be asked the same or a similar question, or a completely different one.

Give full answers, adding relevant comments, reasons, or examples.

Part 2

First compare the two pictures, pointing out similarities and differences.

Then move to the task written above the pictures.

Part 3

First explore each of the issues suggested by the written prompts. Don't be afraid to give opinions and make comments, agreeing or disagreeing with your partner.

Then when reaching a decision, remember there are no right or wrong choices and that you won't be given marks on your opinions but on the language you produce.

Part 4

Answer questions in depth and express your opinions clearly.

Involve your partner in the discussion.

PART 1 (2 minutes)

Tip strip

Celebrations and special occasions

Question 2: Your answer may be 'yes' or 'no', but don't forget to give reasons. For example, you could talk about how you feel on your birthday, what you like to do and who you like to spend it with.

Question 3: Don't spend time thinking about the exact details of a meal you prepared, just talk! Remember that the examiner is only interested in the language you produce. For example, you could talk about whether the meal was a success, where and when it was, and who was invited.

Sport

Question 1: Give examples of activities you do to keep healthy – for example, it could be a sport like running or just walking up the stairs. You can also talk about food and diet, not smoking, etc.

Question 3: If you didn't do any formal sports when you were a child, say why and mention games and physical activities you took part in.

Communication

Question 2: This may be information about people, events, the environment, etc. For example, you could talk about how you like to get information: whether you listen to the news, read newspapers or find the latest news online.

Question 4: You could mention magazines you read about famous people, blogs or tweets. You could give an example of a famous person you like to hear about.

Good morning/afternoon/evening. My name is … and this is my colleague … .

And your names are?

- Where are you from, *(Candidate A)*?
- And you, *(Candidate B)*?

First we'd like to know something about you.

Select one or more questions from any of the following categories, as appropriate.

Celebrations and special occasions

- **What do you usually do to celebrate New Year?**
- **Do you like having a party on your birthday? (Why?/Why not?)**
- **Have you ever cooked a meal for your friends or family?**
- **What entertainment would you usually have at a party with friends?**

Sport

- **What do you do to keep healthy?**
- **Do you like sports competitions? (Why?/Why not?)**
- **Did you play any sports as a child?**
- **Do you prefer playing or watching sports (Why?)**

Communication

- **How often do you use your phone?**
- **Is it important to keep up with what's happening in the world? (Why?/Why not?)**
- **What type of television programme do you like most? (Why?)**
- **Do you like reading about famous people? (Why?/Why not?)**

Candidate A: You could compare the fun and pleasure of sharing a meal with lots of friends with that of sharing photos, messages or gossip with just a few friends. You could refer to *the noisy atmosphere, buying a pizza to save money, not to have to cook and wash up, what the friends in the second photo may be talking about.*

Candidate B: You could compare the quiet environment of the library, which is ideal for studying, with the lively café, the seriousness of the students and the smiling face of the man in the café. You could refer to *how much the students are concentrating, the stress-free experience of reading the paper and enjoying a cup of coffee.*

PART 2 (4 minutes)

In this part of the test, I'm going to give each of you two photographs. I'd like you to talk about your photographs on your own for about a minute, and also to answer a question about your partner's photographs.

(Candidate A), it's your turn first. Here are your photographs. They show **people sharing things with friends**. [*Turn to the pictures on page 49.*] I'd like you to compare the photographs, and say **why you think the people have decided to share**. All right?

(1 minute)

Thank you. *(Candidate B),* **do you like to prepare meals with friends**?

(30 seconds)

Thank you. Now, *(Candidate B),* here are your photographs. They show **people reading**. [*Turn to the pictures on page 50.*] I'd like you to compare the photographs, and say **why you think the people have chosen to read in these places**. All right?

(1 minute)

Thank you. *(Candidate A),* **do you enjoy reading in bed**? (**Why?/Why not?**)

(30 seconds)

For the first part of the task you could say:
I like the idea of going to college or university after school because you can get a better job with a degree.

For the second part:
I think taking a year off to travel is actually very practical and useful for students because they can see the world and perhaps learn a language.

Part 3 (4 minutes)

Now I'd like you to talk about something together for about two minutes.

Some students in their final year at school are thinking about what to do in the future. Here are some of their ideas and a question for you to discuss. First you have some time to look at the task. [*Turn to the task on page 51.*]

(15 seconds)

Now, talk to each other about **why these ideas might be attractive for students who are leaving school.**

(2 minutes)

Thank you. Now you have about a minute to decide **which idea would be most useful for the students' long-term future.**

(1 minute)

Tip strip

Question 1: Possible answers include: *schools could teach more practical skills, invite people with interesting jobs to talk to students, organise visits to work places.*

Question 2: Possible answers include: *you learn new skills, meet interesting people, earn your own money, it may help you decide what work you want in the future.*

Question 3: *You use the language skills you've learnt, experience a different culture and environment, see how other young people study or work.*

Part 4 (4 minutes)

Use the following questions in order, as appropriate:

- **Some people say schools should do more to prepare students for the world of work. What do you think?**

- **Do you think holiday jobs are a good experience for students? (Why?/Why not?)**

- **How important is it for young people to travel to different countries?**

- **How easy do you think it is to decide about your future when you are young?**

- **What would be your ideal job?**

- **Is it difficult for young people to get good jobs nowadays? (Why?/Why not?)**

Select any of the following prompts, as appropriate:

- **What do you think?**
- **Do you agree?**
- **And you?**

Thank you. That is the end of the test.

Practice Test 2

Part 1

For questions **1–8**, read the text below and decide which answer (**A**, **B**, **C** or **D**) best fits each gap. There is an example at the beginning (**0**).

In the exam, you mark your answers **on a separate answer sheet**.

Example:

0 **A** carried   **B** organised   **C** managed   **D** arranged

0	A	B	C	D
	—			

The ideal job

A government research agency recently **(0)** .... out a survey in which 15,000 people in the UK were asked the question: 'What would be your ideal job?' Incredibly, around 60% of those who **(1)** .... in the questionnaire gave the same answer. It may **(2)** .... as a surprise to anyone who actually works in the business, but these people all thought they would like to be writers.

(3) .... no data is available to **(4)** .... their reasons for choosing this particular occupation, it seems that what **(5)** .... to these people is the lifestyle that they imagine a writer leading. Writing work is often done from home, with no **(6)** .... timetable and so can be combined with family commitments and other activities.

In reality, of course, the lifestyle isn't so very glamorous. Most writers work on a freelance **(7)** .... and so have no regular salary to rely on, challenging deadlines are the norm, and only the most successful of them can expect to **(8)** .... a living from it.

1	**A** answered	**B** filled	**C** completed	**D** applied
2	**A** come	**B** sound	**C** result	**D** seem
3	**A** However	**B** Although	**C** Otherwise	**D** Despite
4	**A** account	**B** inform	**C** explain	**D** refer
5	**A** likes	**B** attracts	**C** enjoys	**D** appeals
6	**A** heavy	**B** stuck	**C** fixed	**D** solid
7	**A** basis	**B** method	**C** system	**D** way
8	**A** take	**B** do	**C** have	**D** make

Part 2

For questions **9–16**, read the text below and think of the word which best fits each gap. Use only **one** word in each gap. There is an example at the beginning (**0**).

In the exam, you write your answers **IN CAPITAL LETTERS on a separate answer sheet**.

Example: | **0** | A | S | | | | | | | | | | | | | | | | | | | | |

Measuring time

The idea of the day (**0**) …….. a unit of time is clearly a part of nature. Even the earliest humans must have (**9**) …….. aware that time was divided into alternating periods of light and dark. Exactly when people began to divide the day up into smaller units (**10**) …….. that they could measure time more accurately, however, remains uncertain.

According (**11**) …….. historians, it was the ancient Greeks (**12**) …….. first came up with the idea of the hour, and calculated how many of these made up the typical day. The Greeks are also believed to (**13**) …….. invented the minute, the subdivision of the hour into smaller units.

Generally speaking, the calculations of the ancient scientists have proved remarkably accurate, even (**14**) …….. nature itself isn't always completely regular. Slight variations (**15**) …….. the Earth's orbit around the sun mean that occasional adjustments to measured time are necessary. For example, in 2015 (**16**) …….. is called a leap second was added to official time.

For questions **17–24**, read the text below. Use the word given in capitals at the end of some of the lines to form a word that fits in the gap **in the same line**. There is an example at the beginning (**0**).

In the exam, you write your answers **IN CAPITAL LETTERS on a separate answer sheet**.

Example: | **0** | I | N | V | E | N | T | I | O | N | | | | | | | | | | | | |

Nutella

It is often said that necessity is the mother of (**0**) .... , and this is certainly true of Nutella. In the years after the Second World War, chocolate was a luxury product in Europe that only (**17**) .... rich people could enjoy. Nutella, an (**18**) .... spread made from hazelnuts, was the brainchild of Pietro Ferrero, who saw a gap in the market for a product that could be spread thinly on bread, which was cheap and (**19**) .... at the time.   INVENT

RELATIVE

AFFORD

PLENTY

Hazelnuts grew in (**20**) .... around Alba in northern Italy where Ferrero lived and Nutella soon became popular in Italy, where it was regarded as a (**21**) .... breakfast item, especially for children. This is still true today as the product contains no artificial colours or (**22**) ....   ABUNDANT

HEALTH

PRESERVE

It was never Ferrero's (**23**) .... to sell Nutella as a chocolate substitute, however, and it soon became a worldwide success in its own right. By 2015, an (**24**) .... 365 million tons of Nutella was being consumed annually in 160 countries around the world.   INTEND

CREDIBLE

Part 4

For questions **25–30**, complete the second sentence so that it has a similar meaning to the first sentence, using the word given. **Do not change the word given.** You must use between **two** and **five** words, including the word given. Here is an example (**0**).

Example:

0   What type of music do you like best?

FAVOURITE

What .... type of music?

The gap can be filled with the words 'is your favourite', so you write:

Example: | **0** | | *IS YOUR FAVOURITE* |

In the exam, you write **only** the missing words **IN CAPITAL LETTERS on a separate answer sheet**.

---

25   Not many people have signed up for the trip to London.

NUMBER

Only .... people have signed up for the trip to London.

26   Tommy expected the ride to be more exciting than it actually was.

NOT

The ride .... Tommy had expected.

27   Clea said that she ought to call her father to tell him she was going to be late.

BETTER

'I .... know that I'm going to be late,' said Clea.

28   People say the couple will marry next month.

RUMOURED

The couple .... married next month.

29   She said I had stolen the money.

ACCUSED

She .... the money.

30   A local mechanic services Grace's car.

HAS

Grace .... a local mechanic.

You are going to read an extract from an article about the Olympic Games. For questions **31–36**, choose the answer (**A**, **B**, **C** or **D**) which you think fits best according to the text.

In the exam, you mark your answers **on a separate answer sheet**.

The original Olympic hero

In what is probably the first memorable sporting action photo, we see a tiny man with a moustache, bent backwards, eyes closing in exhaustion, a handkerchief slipping off his head, surrounded by officials as he finishes the marathon at the London Olympics of 1908. The man was Dorando Pietri, an Italian baker. In many ways, this was the beginning of global media coverage for big sporting events, and Pietri became the first global sporting celebrity.

Early last century, when Pietri began running in his home town of Carpi in northern Italy, the ancient Greek idea of the marathon race was just being rediscovered. The course for the London Games was set by Britain's Queen Alexandra, who decided that for her grandchildren's convenience the race should start beneath the nursery window at their home, Windsor Castle. The finish line in London's White City stadium was 26 miles and 385 yards away – which remains the marathon's official distance today.

Back then, the best preparation for running a marathon was believed to be steak for breakfast. Pietri had also taken a chemical called strychnine – today typically used in rat poison – in the mistaken belief that it would improve his performance. By the time he approached White City he understandably felt a little unwell. He later recalled seeing 'a grey mass in front', which proved to be the stadium. He added, 'After that, I remember little.'

line 18

It soon became obvious that Pietri was struggling. He began running the wrong way around the track. When officials pointed this out to him, he fell over. He got up, then collapsed again. Arthur Conan Doyle, creator of *Sherlock Holmes*, was watching from a few metres away, reporting for the *Daily Mail*. He wrote: 'It is horrible, and yet fascinating, this struggle between a set purpose and an utterly exhausted frame.'

The crowd – including Queen Alexandra – began urging the officials to help Pietri. Pietri kept collapsing, but eventually they practically pushed him across the finish line. Conan Doyle was impressed: 'No ancient Roman had known how to accept the laurels of victory better than Pietri.' Seconds after Pietri, the American runner Johnny Hayes, a sales clerk at Bloomingdale's department store in New York, trotted over the line. Quite naturally, Hayes pointed out that Pietri had been helped, which was against the rules. After much debate, Hayes was declared the winner. Pietri fell unconscious, and several newspapers prematurely reported his death.

There is no celebrity without mass media. If you could choose anyone on earth to write up your drama in 1908, it would be Conan Doyle in the *Daily Mail*, which in 1902 had become the bestselling newspaper on earth, with circulation topping one million. Newspapers around the world reprinted Conan Doyle's article. He also started a collection to help Pietri set up his own bakery. Throw in the startling action picture by an unknown photographer, and Pietri's story went global.

What moved the world in 1908 was the sight of an ordinary man attempting something extraordinary. Nowadays people dressed in Donald Duck costumes run double marathons for charity, but in 1908 completing a marathon was considered an almost superhuman feat. To my mind, that distinguishes Pietri from the Olympic heroes of today. Most of them have lived since childhood in a higher realm of top-performance sport. They are better prepared than Pietri in every way, but it is much easier to see ourselves in him.

31 The length of the modern marathon race

    A was based on measurements used in ancient games.

    B used to be changed quite often at the Olympic Games.

    C used to be much longer than it is in the current Games.

    D was originally fixed at the 1908 London Olympic Games.

32 In the third paragraph, the writer suggests that Pietri's preparation for the race

    A had ignored expert advice.

    B hadn't really been appropriate.

    C had been interrupted by illness.

    D had not involved running the course itself.

33 The word 'this' in line 18 refers to

    A Pietri's state of health.

    B an error which Pietri made.

    C an attempt to give Pietri first aid.

    D the correct direction in which Pietri should run.

34 What impressed Sir Arthur Conan Doyle about the end of the race?

    A Pietri's determination to finish it.

    B Pietri's willingness to accept defeat.

    C The way Pietri was helped to complete it.

    D The respect which Pietri showed for the rules.

35 What does the writer suggest in the sixth paragraph?

    A Conan Doyle felt that he had treated Pietri badly.

    B Pietri didn't approve of what was written about him.

    C Pietri benefitted from the fact that Conan Doyle was famous.

    D The photograph of Pietri was more important than the newspaper article.

36 In the final paragraph, the writer expresses

    A admiration for Pietri's attempt at the marathon.

    B surprise that Pietri attracted so much media attention.

    C doubts about the commitment of some modern athletes.

    D disappointment with the way modern marathons are organised.

Part 6

You are going to read an article by a painter about his search for his grandfather's pictures. Six sentences have been removed from the article. Choose from the sentences **A–G** the one which fits each gap (**37–42**). There is one extra sentence you do not need to use.

In the exam, you mark your answers **on a separate answer sheet**.

My grandfather's paintings

My grandfather, Leopold Seyffert, was one of the most famous American portrait painters of the early 20th century. His paintings of personalities from the cultural and business elite made him rich. But as trends in contemporary art changed in the second half of the century, his work went out of fashion. Many of his portraits were lost or stashed away in attics. I've spent years now tracking them down.

It all began one day when I came across one of my grandfather's paintings by chance in a Hollywood antiques shop. It was a portrait of Elsie Whelan, the daughter of a Philadelphia banker, and in perfect condition. **37** After that, I began to wake up in the middle of the night wondering where all his paintings were. Was this one hanging in someone's hallway? Was that one stuffed in a basement or attic? As a painter myself, I see portraits as important social documents, and I developed a desire to seek them out.

All the portraits have stories attached to them. **38** A couple more were in a storage unit in Connecticut – the owner emailed me out of the blue saying she had a bunch of Leopold's stuff. Others I've tracked down online. Because Leopold was such a good technician, his works are typically in great shape. Even if one was painted in 1904, it looks like it was painted in 2014.

My grandfather led an incredible life. He went from being a German immigrant kid without a high-school education to making $68,000 a year during the Great Depression of the 1930s. **39** One day, his boss saw his drawings and said, 'I'll pay for you to go to art school.' Leopold attended the Pennsylvania Academy of the Fine Arts, where he studied with William Merritt Chase.

Leopold died in 1956, a few years after I was born, so we didn't know each other. But I feel a connection to him through my own work. His son, my uncle Richard, was also a successful artist who did portraits of famous people. I knew him well, and he was heavily influenced by his father. **40** A few years ago, I organised an exhibition of all our work that travelled to galleries across the USA.

I'm winding down my hunt for my grandfather's paintings. They're gradually all coming to light now and the Smithsonian Museum has digitised many so that there's a record of them. **41** For example, Leopold's portrait of Francis Ayer of NW Ayer & Son, one of the first advertising companies in America, is sitting in a vault somewhere.

The most recent Leopold work that I acquired is a portrait of Duane Van Vechten, the arts patron. I have it hanging in my studio. It's remarkable. I love saying hello to it when I arrive in the morning and goodbye when I leave. **42** That's what's amazing about these things. There's a human connection, passed down through the years from my grandfather to me.

A Like them, my work – paintings of cities and portraits – is about observing the world around me and expressing that reality in colour.

B He started out as an office boy, sketching people as they came in and out.

C It's like the person is actually there.

D I was thrilled, but it was way out of my price range.

E One was found in a basement at Johns Hopkins University in Baltimore.

F You could say the brush was passed down from Leopold to Richard to myself.

G There are, however, still fifty or so out there somewhere that I'd love to see

Part 7

You are going to read a magazine article about young people who have won prizes for their business ideas. For questions **43–52**, choose from the sections (**A–D**). The sections may be chosen more than once.

In the exam, you mark your answers **on a separate answer sheet.**

Which young person

admits to being over-ambitious initially? | 43 |

enlisted the support of members of the local community? | 44 |

entered a competition in the hope of raising some money? | 45 |

wanted to prove that somebody else was wrong? | 46 |

found some technical aspects of a project rather difficult? | 47 |

gained some useful public attention from the success of a project? | 48 |

received negative feedback on an idea at one stage? | 49 |

was complimented on the originality of an idea? | 50 |

was dissatisfied with an existing service? | 51 |

acknowledges the key contribution of one individual? | 52 |

Young entrepreneurs

We hear from four young people who have won competitions for their business ideas.

A Molly Carluke

My home area is well-known for food and drink, but some local specialities aren't marketed much outside the region. People come here for the seafood, and they're quite taken aback when they get to try the local oatcakes – and that started me thinking. You can buy a similar processed variety in supermarkets, but they don't come up to the standard of the local hand-made ones. I wanted to win the prize because I needed funding to get my idea off the ground. Making oatcakes at home is one thing, but setting up a proper bakery that conforms to all the health-and-safety rules required quite a bit of thought and investment. I think I was aiming too high with the original business plan I drew up, but fortunately my tutor at college was able to bring me down to earth. I'd never have made it without her.

B Ben Barrington

We've always had dogs at home; they play a pretty central role in our lives. But we're also the sort of people who like to travel – and I'm talking about adventure holidays, not a week at the seaside. Anyway, we take the dogs with us whenever we can, but sometimes there's no alternative to putting them in a boarding kennels. We've tried various local ones, but to be honest, we were never particularly comfortable about leaving the dogs at any of them because they looked so messy and disorganised. So my idea was to design a boarding kennel from scratch – with the needs of the dogs as my starting point. My tutor didn't think much of the idea to begin with, because I hadn't really worked out the business side of things – but when I did the research and calculations, both he and I realised that I was onto a winner.

C Adam Luskey

I was pretty sure that there'd be a big demand for a paintballing centre on the island where I live, but the population isn't really big enough to support the investment. That's what I heard when I asked the manager of one company why they hadn't set one up here. They'd tried on a similar island elsewhere, and the costs had been so high that the local kids couldn't afford the entrance fee. I wasn't convinced that he'd got it right however, so I did my own research and put together a business plan. I know that winning the prize doesn't in itself mean that I was right, but it brought my idea to the attention of the island's tourist board, who are willing to help me promote the idea. Doing the plan has made me realise that I have talents that I could develop in other ways.

D Freya Jones

When you're lucky enough live in a place that's both remote and beautiful, you get used to seeing visitors on walking holidays. There's not much to do round here though, so I often wondered how much these people really got out of their visit. That's what gave me the idea of creating audio tours for walkers. I got together people who have lived here all their lives and collected stories of stuff that had happened here over the years, and what to look out for when you're on your walk. Working out how to get good enough recordings without spending a fortune and then how to market the tours online was quite a challenge for me – but the finished product is much more professional than I could ever have imagined. It was my college tutor who suggested I went in for the competition. I didn't think I stood much chance because mine was such a small-scale project, but the judges described it as refreshingly different. Amazing!

Part 1

You **must** answer this question. Write your answer in **140–190** words in an appropriate style.

1   In your English class, you have been talking about the importance of exercise and sport in our daily lives. Now, your English teacher has asked you to write an essay.

Write an essay using **all** the notes and giving reasons for your point of view.

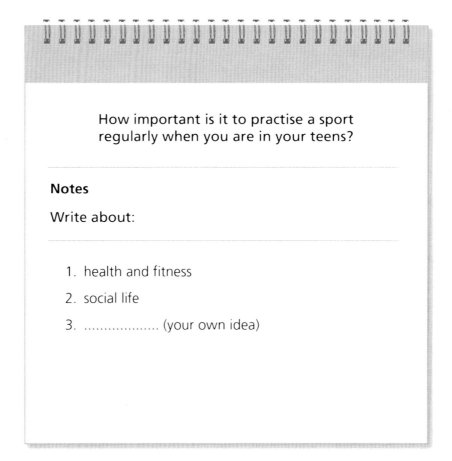

How important is it to practise a sport regularly when you are in your teens?

Notes

Write about:

1. health and fitness

2. social life

3. .... (your own idea)

Part 2

Write an answer to **one** of the questions 2–4 in this part. Write your answer in **140–190** words in an appropriate style.

2   You see this notice in a magazine for students of English.

> ### Write a review for us
> ### and you could see it published in our next issue!
>
> Do you watch programmes for a teenage audience
> on TV or the Internet? Is there one that you particularly like?
>
> Tell us about the programme, what makes it special for you,
> and whether you would recommend it to teenagers and young adults.

Write your **review**.

3   You would like to do some volunteer work in the summer. You have found this leaflet in the Town Hall.

> **We are organising tours for visitors to our town and we need volunteers!**
> **Would you make a good tourist guide for English-speaking tourists?**
>
> - How well do you know our town?
> - Have you any experience of giving tourists information?
> - Do you get on well with people of different ages?
>
> Write a letter telling us why you would make a good guide. Don't forget to include your contact details and to say when you are available. Contact Julia Hadley.

Write your **letter**.

4   Your school has recently opened a new canteen for students. Now your teacher has asked you to write a report, saying what you and your classmates like or dislike about the size and atmosphere, the food and the prices, and making suggestions on how the canteen could be improved.

Write your **report**.

Part 1

You will hear people talking in eight different situations. For questions **1–8**, choose the best answer (**A**, **B** or **C**).

1   You hear two friends talking about a concert they have been to.
    What did the woman like best about it?

    A   the visual impact
    B   the varied programme
    C   the quality of the music

2   You hear a man leaving a voicemail message for a friend.
    Why is he calling?

    A   to give some advice
    B   to answer a question
    C   to ask for clarification

3   You hear two teenagers talking about a new clothes shop.
    What did the girl think of it?

    A   It's very well organised.
    B   It offers good value for money.
    C   It sells a very good range of styles.

4   You overhear two friends talking about playing computer games.
    What do they agree about the games?

    A   They help players develop useful life skills.
    B   They represent an escape from reality.
    C   They prevent players making friends.

5   You hear part of an interview with a trainee chef.
    Why did he decide to apply for his current job?

    A   He wanted to work with top professionals.
    B   He was looking to gain basic experience.
    C   He needed to find a steady income.

6   You hear a college student talking about her course.
    She feels that it should offer more

    A   online support with homework tasks.
    B   practical experience in the workplace.
    C   opportunities to work together with classmates.

7   You hear part of an interview with a football player after a match.
    How does he feel now?

    A   upset about the way he was treated
    B   disappointed with his own performance
    C   angry about the attitude of the other team's players

8   You hear a fashion model talking about her work.
    She feels that some media reports from fashion shows

    A   focus too much on particular models.
    B   fail to recognise the skill of the models.
    C   are unfairly critical of certain models.

Part 2

You will hear an archaeology student called Gina Burbage talking about how she first became interested in the subject as a teenager. For questions **9–18**, complete the sentences with a word or short phrase.

Gína Burbage: Archaeology student

Gina first got involved in the Timescale Project at the suggestion of her

(9) ....

Gina's garden was selected for the project because there used to be a

(10) .... nearby.

Before the day of the dig, Gina studied a book of

(11) .... to find out more about her village.

Gina compares the geophysical survey to an

(12) .... to give us an idea of how it works.

The geophysical survey showed the position of an old

(13) .... in Gina's garden.

The first object found in Gina's garden was a

(14) .... dating from the nineteenth century.

The first piece of pottery found in Gina's garden dated from the

(15) .... century.

Gina was very excited when a **(16)** .... from the Roman period was found in her garden.

Gina collected a total of **(17)** .... pieces of pottery from the hole she dug in her garden.

Gina uses the word **(18)** ....
to explain how she felt at the end of the day.

Part 3

You will hear five short extracts in which students are talking about doing a period of work experience in a company as part of their course. For questions **19–23**, choose from the list (**A–H**) what each speaker liked best about the experience. Use the letters only once. There are three extra letters which you do not need to use.

A   working in a range of departments

Speaker 1   19

B   getting to deal with the public

Speaker 2   20

C   being given real responsibility

Speaker 3   21

D   having a good range of tasks

Speaker 4   22

E   making useful contacts

Speaker 5   23

F   learning relevant skills

G   seeing how problems are solved

H   understanding how systems work

Part 4

You will hear part of an interview with a student called Ben Broadley, who is talking about his idea for creating more open spaces for people to use in cities. For questions **24–30**, choose the best answer (**A**, **B** or **C**).

24 Ben's research project on local parks focused on

    A why they were created.

    B how much they have changed.

    C who makes use of them nowadays.

25 What does Ben tell us about UK city parks in the 20th century?

    A houses were often built on them

    B there was less need for them

    C no new ones were created

26 Ben was surprised to discover that in the UK in the 21st century

    A people prefer to live in apartment blocks.

    B fewer homes with gardens are being built.

    C only richer people can afford to have gardens.

27 What does Ben suggest about city-centre parks today?

    A There isn't enough money available to maintain them properly.

    B The people who use them fail to treat them with respect.

    C The facilities available in them tend to be rather old-fashioned.

28 The aim of Ben's 'garden-sharing' scheme is to

    A make better use of private gardens.

    B ensure younger families have the biggest gardens.

    C force owners of large gardens to let other people use them.

29 In order to use a garden in Ben's scheme, families have to

    A pay the owners for time spent in it.

    B buy some equipment to use in it.

    C help the owners to look after it.

30 What has surprised Ben about the scheme?

    A how few problems there have been overall

    B how many garden owners wanted to take part

    C how little damage there has been done to gardens

PART 1 (2 minutes)

Good morning/afternoon/evening. My name is … and this is my colleague … .

And your names are?

- Where are you from, *(Candidate A)*?
- And you, *(Candidate B)*?

First we'd like to know something about you.

Select one or more questions from any of the following categories, as appropriate.

Education and work

- What's the most difficult subject you've ever had to study? (Why?)
- Have you ever done any work as a volunteer, without pay?
- Do you like to have a snack while you study?
- Have you any idea what job you might want to do in the future?

Everyday life

- Tell us what you do when you get home from school/work at the end of the day.
- Which room in your house is the best place to relax?
- Who do you normally spend your weekends with? (What are your plans for this weekend?)
- How much time do you spend helping to keep your house clean and tidy?

Entertainment

- Do you ever go to the cinema or watch films on TV? Tell us about something you saw recently.
- What's your favourite sport? (How often do you play?)
- How often do you go out with friends? (What do you do?)
- Do you prefer to have short breaks or long holidays? (Why?)

In this part of the test, I'm going to give each of you two photographs. I'd like you to talk about your photographs on your own for about a minute, and also to answer a question about your partner's photographs.

(Candidate A), it's your turn first. Here are your photographs. They show **people giving advice**. [*Turn to the pictures on page 52.*] I'd like you to compare the photographs, and say **why you think the people might be giving advice**. All right?
(1 minute)

Thank you. *(Candidate B),* **do you ever give advice to people**?
(30 seconds)

Thank you. Now, *(Candidate B),* here are your photographs. They show **people starting a trip**. [*Turn to the pictures on page 53.*] I'd like you to compare the photographs, and say **how you think the people may be feeling at the start of their trip**. All right?
(1 minute)

Thank you. *(Candidate B),* **do you like going on long trips**? (**Why?/Why not?**)
(30 seconds)

Now I'd like you to talk about something together for about two minutes.

Here are some activities that you can do on your own or with others, and a question for you to discuss. First you have some time to look at the task. [*Turn to the task on page 54.*]

(15 seconds)

Now talk to each other about **whether you think you would get better results by doing these activities on your own or with other people.**

(2 minutes)

Thank you. Now you have about a minute to decide **which activity is best done with other people.**

(1 minute)

Use the following questions in order, as appropriate:

*   Some people say it's impossible to concentrate when there's noise around you. What do you think?

*   Do you think teenagers should be allowed to go everywhere alone? (Why?/Why not?)

*   How important is it for young people to be able to buy fashionable clothes?

*   Which team sport do you like best? (Why?)

*   How important is it to help people who are finding something difficult?

*   What's more important, taking part in a competition or winning it? (Why?)

Thank you. That is the end of the test.

Select any of the following prompts, as appropriate:

*   **What do you think?**
*   **Do you agree?**
*   **And you?**

Visuals for Speaking Tests

Test 1: Part 2, Student A

Why have the people decided to share?

Why have the people chosen to read in these places?

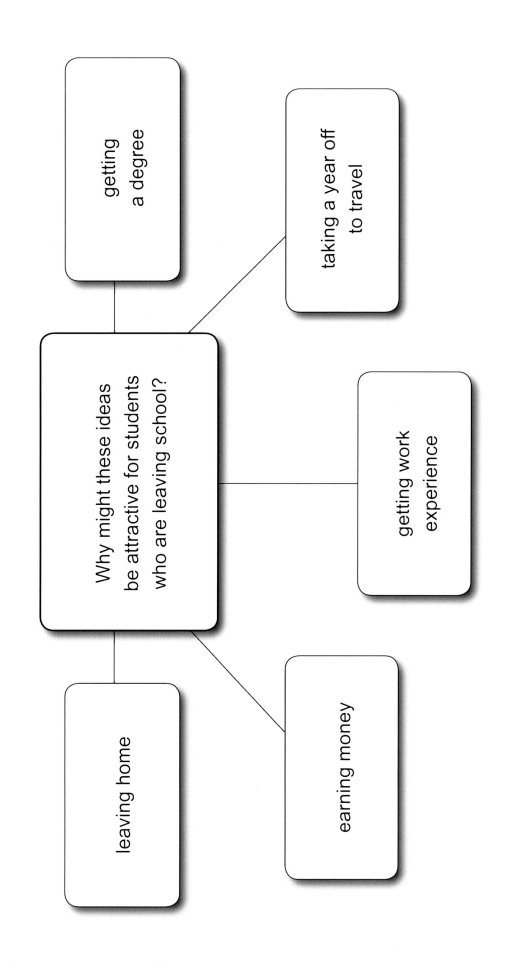

getting a degree

taking a year off to travel

Why might these ideas be attractive for students who are leaving school?

getting work experience

leaving home

earning money

Why are the people giving advice?

How are the people feeling at the start of their trip?

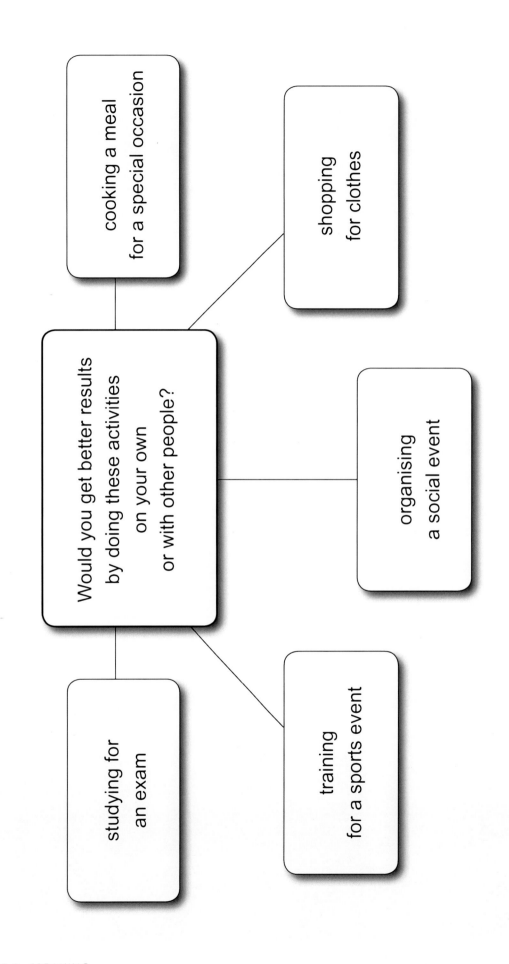

cooking a meal
for a special occasion

shopping
for clothes

Would you get better results
by doing these activities
on your own
or with other people?

organising
a social event

studying for
an exam

training
for a sports event

Speaking and Writing Banks

Part 1

In this part of the test, you answer a few questions on personal topics such as your home, your daily routine, your work, likes and dislikes, etc.

Useful language

Communicative strategies

Sorry, can you say that again?

Sorry, I didn't quite catch that.

Do you mean ...?

Well, that would depend on ...

Well, that's an interesting question.

Oh, yes, definitely/very much so.

No, I'm afraid I don't.

Absolutely!

Now, how can I put this?

Giving personal information

I like to keep in touch with friends. That's why my phone is indispensable.

I've always (dis)liked ... . I'm not sure why.

To be honest, I'm not very good at cooking, but last week I managed to ...

My house is rather small but very comfortable.

I'm an only child and I live with my parents.

Responding to questions about everyday life and interests

Although I love sport, I don't practise any regularly because ...

I'm expected to do some housework; we all have to help out.

I've never done any voluntary work, but I'd love to get involved because ...

I haven't made a final decision yet, but I'd really like to ... in the future.

I'm not very sure what I'll do, but I may decide to ...

My parents want me to ...

I used to be very keen on ... , but now ...

I don't like ..., really, though I do enjoy ...

Exam help

- You know the answer to these questions, so reply confidently and add interesting information.

- Avoid making basic grammar mistakes. Think about the verb tense you are going to use: is the question about the past, the present or the future?

- Activate the vocabulary area of the question. For example, if the question is about your favourite type of TV programme, think of comedies, soap operas, news, quizzes, etc.

- Speak clearly so that your partner and the two examiners can understand everything you say.

Part 2

In this part of the test, you speak on your own for one minute. You compare two photographs and answer a question about them.

Useful language

Comparing

The people in these photos are in very different places.

In the first photo they're … , whereas in the second …

These are very different activities …

These are very different ways of …

I can see some similarities in these photos, for example, the people in both pictures are friends …

This first photo is more/less attractive than the second because …

The man in the café seems to be having a better time than …

There's a clear difference between these two photos; one of them is … whilst the other …

I don't think the people in the first photo are as happy as those in the second.

Speculating

I may be wrong, but I'd say these are probably close friends.

We don't know what they're looking at, but I suppose …

Perhaps they've decided to share this because …

The people seem to be enjoying each other's company.

I get the impression that the woman …

The girl looks like she's feeling …

He may have chosen to read here because …

I think the girl looks really tired, she may have been studying all day.

The people in the first photo are probably …

I think this person may be under a lot of stress because …

Exam help

- Remember that you have not been asked to describe the photos but to compare them. There is no time to comment in detail on one photo at a time. Start off by comparing the people, the places and the situations and give a personal reaction to the pictures.

- Use the question written above the photos to remind yourself that after you have compared the photos, you have to do the second task. In the second part, you are asked to speculate, i.e., to say what you think and give opinions.

- Use varied vocabulary and try to use comparative forms correctly.

- Don't stop to search for a word you don't remember, explain what you want to say in a different way.

Part 3

In this part of the test, you complete a task with your partner. You both initiate discussion of the different written prompts in turn, and respond to each other's comments.

Useful language

Inviting your partner's opinion and taking turns

Some of these ideas don't seem very practical. What do you think?

I don't know about you, but in my opinion students would need …

Shopping for clothes is something I'd definitely hate to do on my own. Would you agree with that?

You may disagree with me, but I think you have to study on your own to concentrate properly.

What do you think? Is this a better option?

Why do you think this is a good option?

Following up on your partner's opinions

I'm sure that's something most students would like to do.

As I see it, it would be a waste of time.

Well, in my opinion, getting a degree should be a priority.

That's an interesting point, but we also need to consider …

That's a very good point, but don't you think it might be advisable to …?

As you said, taking a year off is an attractive option. However, …

I take your point, but I still think they'd need to think about other options.

I'm afraid I don't agree. I strongly believe that …

Well, I'd say that …

Moving to another written prompt

Right, why don't we talk about …?

How about this idea? Do you want to say something about it?

Now, moving on, we haven't talked about … yet.

Shall we discuss the option of looking for a job next?

We've probably said enough about this idea, don't you think?

Exam help

- Focus on the two parts of the task you have been given, which requires you to discuss the options for about two minutes. To remind yourself of the task, look back at the question printed in the central box.

- Remember that after the two-minute discussion, you will be given a one-minute decision-making task. Don't come to a decision too soon because you may then struggle to find other things to say.

- When your partner gives an opinion on a written prompt, respond fully before moving to something else. It does not matter if you do not discuss all the prompts, what is important is that you produce sufficient language at the right level.

- If your partner seems happy to let you do the talking, do involve him/her by asking his/her opinions. You will be given credit for doing that.

Part 4

In this part of the test, you take part in a discussion by answering questions which broaden the topic of Part 3. You can also respond to what your partner says.

Useful language

Giving opinions

Well, personally, I feel …

People often say that … , but I …

Young people often complain that … and I agree.

I don't think teenagers should be prevented from doing things.

I'd do something different …

I think it's unlikely that anybody would …

Yes, I think young people have much more freedom than …

I think they find it really difficult to decide …

No, that's not the way I see things.

I'm not sure to be honest.

My family think I am wrong, but I believe …

Let's be optimistic about the future and say that …

Buying the latest fashion is out of the question if you have little money.

Giving examples and/or reasons

I can think of a few examples of this …

Let me try to explain why …

For example, when you ….

I once had an experience which…

To clarify what I mean, I can give you …

There are many reasons for this …

People dislike this idea. I think this is because …

When you're young you can be adventurous. That's why I …

Just think of all the challenges young people face; to begin with …

Exam help

- Remember these questions require more extended responses than those in Part 1. Don't be afraid to talk about your opinions and feelings. The examiner only wants you to produce some complex language to show off your level.

- There is no 'correct' answer to the questions and you will not be assessed on what you think, but you should always give reasons and back up your opinions.

- You are encouraged to contribute ideas to what your partner says, even if the question was not addressed to you.

- You have now warmed up and this is the last part of your test. Enjoy the interaction and the feeling that you can express your ideas with confidence!

Part 1: Essay

Sample answer (see task on page 19)

Useful language

Useful language

Introduction

You often hear people say that ...

There are arguments for and against this idea.

People often disagree as to whether it is ...

This is an important topic that needs to be discussed ...

Speculative language

They may attract attention on social media.

They could be unfairly criticised ...

They might be subjected to attacks.

Some unhappiness may be hidden ...

Conclusion

To sum up, I will say that ...

Taking all this into account, I believe ...

Having discussed different points of view, it seems clear that ...

Finally, I have come to the conclusion that ...

Exam help

- Read the question carefully and plan what you want to include in four or five clear paragraphs. (See the suggested essay plan on page 60.)

- Write down some interesting ideas for each paragraph, together with some language you may want to use. You will need to use varied vocabulary relevant to the topic and some complex sentences using linking words.

- Remember that you are presenting your point of view and you need to back it up with some reasons or evidence.

- Make sure you use a formal or semi-formal style and avoid the use of informal language.

How easy or difficult is life for people who suddenly become celebrities?

When somebody becomes a celebrity more or less overnight, their life will change. Some changes will be positive, some negative.

First of all, celebrity status usually means lots of money, as celebrities get innumerable offers of work to appear on television and promote and advertise luxury goods. Having so much wealth may seem like a dream, but it could cause problems such as false friends who are only interested in their money.

Secondly, there is the unavoidable loss of privacy. Celebrities are recognised in the street, so they are not able to hide anywhere. People will ask them for autographs and want to take selfies with them. Whilst some people love that sort of attention, others may find it unbearable, particularly if it also affects their families.

Finally, celebrities may attract negative attention and comments on social media, where they could be unfairly criticised or subjected to attacks. They may even become the object of envy and hatred.

To sum up, it seems to me that celebrities lead a life of luxury and receive a lot of public attention, but we often don't see how much unhappiness may be hidden behind the happy exterior.

Using linking words such as 'secondly' or 'finally' will help you to organise the ideas in your essay.

Use one paragraph for each topic.

Use varied language and some complex sentences.

Your conclusion should be a summary of the opinions you have expressed earlier.

Aim to write five paragraphs

Paragraph 1

The introduction: Try to write two sentences to avoid a single-sentence paragraph. The first sentence can be a re-phrasing of the essay title. The second sentence can be a brief summary of what you are going to say.

Paragraph 2

Deal with the first note: a life of luxury.

Paragraph 3

Deal with the second note: lack of privacy.

Paragraph 4

Deal with the third note (your own): being criticised on social media.

Paragraph 5

The conclusion. Summarise the main points mentioned in paragraphs 2, 3 and 4. Try to write at least two sentences to avoid a single-sentence paragraph.

Each note will be just a few words long. The note on its own will not give you sufficient material. Before you start writing, take a few minutes to expand them. Here is a way to do it:

1   Write down the notes (including your own) and draw three lines from each one. Now concentrate on each note in turn. Try to think of three ideas that can add content to that note. For example:

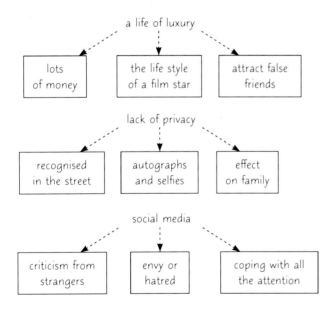

a life of luxury

| lots of money | the life style of a film star | attract false friends |

lack of privacy

| recognised in the street | autographs and selfies | effect on family |

social media

| criticism from strangers | envy or hatred | coping with all the attention |

2   Choose the best ideas from your notes and start writing.

When you have finished writing your essay, use this checklist.

Content

Have you covered the two notes given and one of your own?

Communicative achievement

Is your style correct for an essay, i.e. is it fairly formal? Are your opinions easy to follow?

Organisation

Have you divided your writing into paragraphs, with an introduction and a conclusion?

Language

Have you used:

*   some complex sentences using linking words?
*   a variety of grammatical structures and tenses?
*   some interesting vocabulary?

Part 2: Article

Sample answer (see task on page 20)

You can use direct or indirect questions to add interest.

This engages the readers by addressing them directly.

This is a clear way to introduce the second point you have to include.

Take action to beat stress now!

Give your article a catchy title to attract attention.

▶ Do you find yourself getting more and more anxious while studying? Read on because this page may change your life!

The first thing is to organise your work. This is how I do it: I divide my work into manageable chunks, so that a task that seems enormous becomes a series of smaller tasks. Think of the question: 'How do you eat an elephant?' Well, what's the answer? The answer is 'bit by bit'. Simple and so clever!

▶ The next step: relaxation. It's not enough just to say, 'I'll relax for a few minutes'. You have to take relaxation seriously! Think of an activity that gives you real pleasure. In my case, this means taking a piece of dark chocolate and going into the greenest part of my garden, where I can hear bird song, and eating it slowly, enjoying every moment. Let it clear your head of all thoughts.

And finally, one more tip: share the burden of studying! Invite a friend you get on really well with – it must be somebody who is on the same wave length as you. Discuss the difficult points of your work and give each other lots of support.

Good luck!

Useful language

Rhetorical questions

Do you find yourself getting anxious …?

How would you answer this question?

Are you ready for change? Then …

How about doing something that will change your life?

Addressing the reader directly

Read on because this may change your life!

Share the burden of studying!

You have to take relaxation seriously!

Think of this question.

Giving examples from personal experience

This is how I do it.

In my case this means going …

Personally, I prefer to …

I can say this from experience …

Exam help

- Read the question carefully and plan your article before you start to write. Pay attention to who you are writing this article for. If it is for your school magazine, you may use an informal style. If it is for a magazine with a wider readership, you may need a semi-formal style.

- Write down some interesting language that you may want to use. Remember that the purpose of your article is not only to inform but also to entertain the reader.

- Think of an interesting title.

- Use interesting details, examples or anecdotes to ensure that your article has a personal touch.

Part 2: Email

Sample answer (see task on page 20)

Hi Jack,

Great to hear from you! Your presentation sounds very interesting and I'm happy to be able to help you. ◄----

> Use an informal opening and informal language.

In my country, teenagers go out in the evening most weekends, usually to parties, to friends' houses and sometimes to a disco or club. They go out without any adults, but they're usually expected to come back home by 1 a.m. at the latest, and they have to have a phone so parents can contact them if necessary.

> Divide your email into clear paragraphs.

> You can give examples from your own experience.

You also asked about money. Most teenagers get some pocket money weekly and some save it up for something special they want to buy. Others, like me, spend it very quickly and are soon out of pocket! Many teenagers do jobs like washing neighbours' cars or cutting the grass to earn some extra money.

As to your question about obeying parents, that's more difficult to answer. Some parents are very strict. My parents have some rules I have to obey, but they also give me a lot of space. Some of my friends, however, think their parents are too old-fashioned and don't understand them, so there may be arguments at home.

> Use linking words to produce some complex sentences.

Good luck with your presentation!

Write again soon,

Pat

Useful language

Informal openings
Dear Jack,
Hello Jack,
Hi Jack,

Introducing a new point
You also asked about …
Now, to answer your question about …
As to your question about money, …
Moving on to your question about …
Finally, you wanted to know …

Agreeing to help
I'm happy to be able to help …
I'll do my best to help you …
I'm not an expert but …
I can help you by looking up more …

Wishing good luck
Good luck with your presentation!
I hope your presentation goes really well!
Let me know how your presentation goes!
I'm sure your presentation will be a success!

Exam help

- Read the instructions and the email very carefully, noting down all the information you need to include.
- Decide what to include in each paragraph and jot down some vocabulary you may want to use.
- Try to write close to the maximum number of words.

Part 2: Report

Sample answer (see task on page 20)

> *In the first paragraph, say what the purpose of your report is.*

> *The use of headings allows you to organise the sections of your report clearly.*

> *Try to use some complex sentences by using linking words.*

Report on the Transport Museum

In this report I will talk about the displays, about my classmates' opinions and I'll explain how the visit helped us with our school work.

The displays

There was an amazing number of things to see, from tiny models of old cars and trains to huge ship models you could actually walk inside. There was a room where you could admire the bikes used by world champions together with all the medals they'd won.

What we liked most

We particularly liked the street which had been reconstructed to look like a city street from a century ago, with cars, trams, buses and carriages pulled by horses. It was so well done that you could imagine you were walking there a hundred years ago.

Usefulness of the visit

What we learnt will be really useful for our history projects. Throughout the museum there were large touch screens full of images and films about the displays. These were about transport but also about how the people who used it lived and how they spent their free time.

To conclude, I would say that this was an excellent museum and that we hope all students will be able to see it.

> *Include a final sentence or two summarising your views.*

Useful language

Introducing the report

In this report I will …

The aim/purpose of this report is to …

I have been asked to write a report about …

Stating preferences

We particularly liked …

We were most impressed by …

The display that stood out most was …

The best display by far was …

Finishing the report

Having looked at all the displays, I can say that …

To conclude, I would say that …

Taking into account everything we saw, I conclude that …

The main conclusion of my report is that …

Exam help

- Read the question carefully and plan your report before you start to write. Think of the format you are going to use and whether you are going to use headings. Decide how many headings or paragraphs you will need and make a quick calculation of the number of words you can use under each.

- Try to write no fewer than 180 words, but don't get carried away and write too much under one heading.

- Remember you have to show a range of language, so use interesting vocabulary and write full sentences, linking some of your ideas to produce some complex sentences.

- Include a conclusion, even if it is short.

- Check that you have used a semi-formal or formal style and correct any informal language you may have used.

Part 2: Review

Sample answer (see task on page 41)

If you want a show that is both interesting and funny, look no further. 'Simple Things' is about Robin, a teenager, and his friends. Robin is no ordinary teenager, he is someone with a wicked sense of humour who can play the drums. The plot is about his attempts to become a pop star whilst helping his friends solve their problems.

What makes it so special for me? I love the humour in it. Whatever the problems, the different characters always have a positive, upbeat message. And Robin's jokes are so funny they never fail to make me laugh. You feel that you are there with them, laughing in the same room.

And there's something else. There is humour but also drama and tension between the characters. It's often helped me understand my own problems better because some of the characters are such good role models. I often ask myself, 'What would I do in that situation? Would I do what Robin does?'

If you're over 20, forget it. But I'd recommend it without hesitation to anybody between 15 and 19. But I must warn you, it's so good it can become addictive!

> Use your imagination! You can invent things like the name or content of the programme.

> Always give examples to back up your opinions.

> Don't be afraid to express your personal views.

> Don't forget that you will need a couple of lines at the end for the last requirement of the task.

Sample answer (see task on page 41)

Useful language

Introducing the plot

This is about …

This tells the story of a boy …

We learn about the relationships …

This programme takes the viewer to …

The programme is set in … (time/place)

Expressing enthusiasm

I love the humour in this …

It never fails to amuse me …

You won't believe how good this is …

It's so good it can become addictive …

Recommending

I'd recommend this without hesitation …

If you want to…, look no further.

I wouldn't recommend this to anyone over the age of …

If you like comedies, this show is definitely for you.

Exam help

- Read the question carefully and plan your review before you start to write. Think of the style you will use, which will probably be semi-formal.

- Think about how you will organise the content into paragraphs. You need to deal with several tasks within the question: to inform the reader about the programme, to give your personal opinion and to say whether you would recommend it.

- You will need to use varied language, including interesting adjectives. Jot down some words you may want to use so that you can avoid the overuse of words such as 'good' or 'nice'.

- Check your spelling and punctuation and correct any basic errors you may have made.